Life Edge

Leading, Managing And Developing Yourself

Pete Rogan and Stuart Rogan

978-1-917728-07-2

Copyright © Pete Rogan and Stuart Rogan 2025

All rights reserved.

All intellectual property rights including copyright, design right and publishing rights rest with the author. No part of this book may be reproduced or transmitted in any way including any written, electronic, recording, or photocopying without written permission of the author. The information contained within and views expressed in this memoir are those of the author and those who freely contributed their recollections to the author.

Published in Ireland by Orla Kelly Publishing.

Orla Kelly Publishing,
27 Kilbrody,
Mount Oval,
Rochestown,
Cork,
Ireland.

'Life Edge' is dedicated to Chris Maxwell, with thanks for the unending powerhouse insights, ideas, challenges, inspiration, friendship and support across many years, many subjects and many phases of life. Boom!

We'd like to note our sincere thanks to our publisher Orla Kelly, our editor Tim Turner, and our graphic designer Kevin Lloyd, whose diligence, care, patience and forbearance have been instrumental in bringing this book to life.

Who This Book is For

'Life Edge' is a practical guide designed to help you unlock your potential and achieve success in both your personal and professional life. With actionable strategies and easy-to-follow frameworks, it offers tools that can be immediately applied to real-life challenges.

Whether you're looking to excel in your career, build better habits, or find clarity in your goals, this book provides a step-by-step approach to growth. With relatable examples and proven techniques, 'Life Edge' is tailored for anyone seeking sustainable, meaningful change.

So if you struggle with:

- Finding direction or purpose in your life or career.
- Transforming your ambitions into actionable, measurable goals.
- Staying motivated and disciplined to see projects through to the end.
- Learning how to balance goal-oriented focus and achievements with emotional wellbeing.
- Developing frameworks for self-leadership and personal growth.

And want:

- Actionable insights.
- A practical guide and a time-tested self-management system..
- To develop habits that provide lifelong personal and professional benefits.

Then 'Life Edge' is for you!

About the Authors

Pete and Stuart Rogan

Pete Rogan, co-author of 'Life Edge' and founder of Future Positive Consulting is an organisational psychologist and seasoned expert with 35 years of experience across personal development, management development and business improvement. Together with his son Stuart, managing director and co-author, they have worked with individuals from diverse industries and backgrounds, honing a deep understanding of the challenges people face in navigating their personal and professional journeys.

Their pragmatic approach and commitment to developing a holistic, coherent system for lifelong personal development ensures that every framework and tool presented in the book is time-tested, practical, and impactful.

Contents

Who This Book is For	v
About the Authors.	vii
Pete's story.	xi
Stuart's story	xiv
Client Testimonials	xvii
Introduction:.	1
Overview	7
Part One: Leading, Managing And Developing Yourself – Key Concepts	11
Part Two: How To.	27
Part Three: Making It Work For You.	47
Next Steps.	53
Bonus Items	57
More From Life Edge	58
About Future Positive Consulting.	60
Bibliography.	62

Pete's story

"There I was one night, just a normal guy. And there I was the next night. Goddamn, I was still just a normal guy." (**Bruce Springsteen**)

Wednesday June 5th, 1985. St James' Park, Newcastle. Springsteen. Born in the U.S.A. tour. I've just turned 25. Life is okay. Bar a vague sense that something's missing.

Bruce introduces 'Racing in the street'. He observes that at 35, he sees some of his friends beginning to *"let the best of themselves slip away"*. That hit me. *"Everyone should have something in their life that they can be proud of,"* he continued. Me? Not especially. Strike two. Into the song: *"Some guys they just give up living, and start dying little by little, piece by piece. Some guys come home from work and wash up and go racing in the street."* Boom! Something clicks into place.

Back at work. Paul is trying to get a team together for a 10-mile charity road race. No thanks. Among other things, I run like a bag of spanners. And I don't feel that I'm cut out for, well, anything. I'm also anxious. About, well, everything.

But, inspired by my newfound need for a noble purpose, I signed up. Donned the bandana. Got to work. Trained hard.

Some weeks later. Got round. Before dark. Not dead. Finished first in our wee team. Bloody hell! What else?

A half-marathon? Month later. Done. A marathon. Surely not? Two months later. Done. The New York Marathon. People like me don't do that. What the hell.1986. Done.

Now what? I was an engineer. Not a very good one. I had harboured a fantasy about a switch to psychology. Oh, and I'd love to play guitar, write songs, start my own business and write a book. But that doesn't happen. Not to people like me. Or at least, not to me.

Long story short. Some years later, I've run over 100 marathons and 500 half-marathons. I have a first-class honours in psychology. And two master's degrees. Moved into training, then management, then consultancy. Then set up in business. Been in business 27 years. Paid the bills. Had some wonderful adventures and unforgettable moments. Worked with some outstanding people and organisations. Written and recorded 200 really terrible (unreleased) songs (you're safe). Published author. Reduced the grip that anxiety and insecurity had on me. Helped bring up my son (co-author Stuart). I now have a 30-year plan that fills me with energy and excitement. (While keenly aware that my allotted span might be 30 minutes.) There's just so much to learn and contribute.

So, while I'm not exactly, well, Bruce Springsteen, the distance I've travelled and the difference it has made to my life is beyond what I ever thought was possible.

But why am I boring you with this? Well, fired up by Bruce's challenge, I got interested in, and picked up on, all sorts of literature, tools, mentors and sources of information, ideas and inspiration. I gradually developed my own system for managing and developing myself. Used it, shared it, refined it, honed it and consolidated it (still doing so).

It's helped me, Stuart, and many clients to unlock more of their potential, uncover hitherto unseen possibilities and get closer to the rewards that their time and talents merit.

And I'd like to share it with you now in the hope that it might fire you up, guide you and keep you going through the challenges to unfold your talents, unlock opportunities, reach some unforgettable, life-enhancing moments and achievements that you might not otherwise have, and, above all, to enjoy the great adventure of life.

Stuart's story

Like father like son, I too had a seminal moment at a Bruce Springsteen concert. For me, it was July 19th, 2008 in the Nou Camp Stadium, Barcelona. The evening air, the music, the 70,000 people sharing a moment combined to make a transcendent experience. The moment was vivid, and the feeling lasted well beyond the show. At nine years old, this was an intense insight into the peak experiences that life can bring, and so triggered my lifelong interest in what it means to live fully, with vitality, and to make a positive contribution to other people's lives through one's work and relationships.

Sensing that my musical skill was no match for Springsteen's, I would have to find a different vehicle for my work! At age 10 I took the opportunity to start a very early apprenticeship with the family consulting business. My Dad began by arranging for me to meet and learn from various leaders in business. One CEO, named Ray, stood out. The character, dynamism and vision that he shared immediately resonated and got me excited by the power of an excellently run organisation to enhance lives.

With a growing sense that my pursuit of choice would be to help individuals and organisations achieve excellence, I set about developing my capability. To this end, through my teens I sought to equip myself with the broadest possible education in life and business. This took me from farmyards to boardrooms while pursuing an understanding of the most prevalent management theories and philosophies, the principles of effective self-management, and a rudimentary understanding of many things such as psychology, world history, the sciences, the arts and pretty much anything else that might help to enlighten and guide us towards living enriched lives and making an informed, positive contribution to the future.

In 2020 I published my first book, titled The Gift. I had developed a close friendship with my grandfather, and we talked at length about his life, from abject childhood poverty to owner of a successful small business via six years of fighting in the British army. He fought every day of the Second World War, most notably as a gunner at El-Alamein, one of history's most pivotal battles and where the first reverse was inflicted on Nazi land forces, prompting Winston Churchill's famous "…it is, perhaps, the end of the beginning" remark. After my grandfather's death I was inspired to write about the legacy of his, the 'greatest' generation; their values, the hard lessons they learned and what the generations of today can learn from them to lead more balanced lives and leave a positive legacy of their own.

In 2016, I officially joined Future Positive, becoming managing director in 2022. During my time with the business, we have worked with clients in tech, luxury goods, pharmaceuticals, engineering and food retail distribution and partnered with prominent business schools to develop our comprehensive, field-tested, proprietary toolkit for improving business strategy, operational performance and culture. We've also worked with many individual clients on matters of personal or professional development, their ages ranging from 19 to 84.

After thousands of conversations on developing people and organisations, we've observed some fundamentals that seem to be true for all those with a hunger to develop themselves. As you're reading this book, you probably have a desire to experience and express the best of yourself, even if you don't quite know what that means. You probably also face an array of doubts and distractions that risk derailing you from this without strong values, a vision to work towards, and an ecology of habits to keep you positive, proactive, and connected to the best of yourself through the rigours and tumult of life.

Though the journey to unlock one's potential will never be fully complete, 'Life Edge' is a distillation of the tools, concepts and practices that we have found to be the most impactful for our clients and for ourselves. I hope you enjoy 'Life Edge', and that it goes some way to helping you be the best you can be.

Client Testimonials

'Life Edge' has helped me to manage my time and utilise my talents. In just nine weeks I've been able to gain focus and develop new habits that have helped me to achieve tangible results. I've rebranded my business, increased sales and improved how I serve my customers. All while getting more time for exercise and relaxation. It's been transformational."

Callum

"Practical and results oriented. Before this programme I struggled to set clear goals and take decisive action. 'Life Edge' has allowed me to clarify a clear vision of what I want to achieve and to develop the skills and focus needed to set goals and routinely achieve them. I'm more confident, more action-focused, have made significant progress in my career and with other important wider-life projects and am firmly on course to achieve my long-term ambitions."

Sigridur

"Working with Future Positive has been an inspiration. It has helped me explore and find ways forward with things I wanted to do for ages but never quite had the confidence to fully commit to. The Life-Edge programme has also provided exactly the practical support I need to stay focused, on track, and consistently delivering on what I said I would do."

Joe

"I undertook professional development training with Future Positive and couldn't recommend it more. The direct and engaging way Stuart handled the session gave me the confidence to be ambitious and innovative when designing my development plan. I have been through other professional development sessions but this was unique in the way it challenged me to strive for more, whilst providing me with the tools to be able to achieve my ambitions......... Definitely get in touch with FP if you want to get more out of your days, career and life."

Oliver

"The straightforward and pragmatic approach of 'Life Edge' has been pivotal. The goal setting pack has inspired me to think big and to create a long-term career plan in line with my values, while with the weekly accountability I've been able to see an increase in my productivity at work and achieve a major breakthrough with my personal fitness – by running my first half-marathon."

Graeme

"Working with Future Positive has transformed my approach to development, with a new emphasis on harnessing my strengths and focusing on the positive. Stuart could not have been more generous with his time and the one-to-one sessions on DISC, personal strategy and performance management has not only led to a huge leap in my capability to deliver for my team, but also guided my approach to planning my career. I would not be where I am today without Future Positive and cannot recommend Pete and Stuart highly enough."

Scott

Introduction

Getting The Best From Yourself And Achieving The Rewards Your Time And Talent Deserve

"Even though we all have the same number of hours in the day and days in the year, some people accomplish great things, during their life, while others achieve only mediocrity." **(Harald Harung)**

Making the best of yourself, putting your talents to good use and living an enjoyable and productive life is, arguably, one's primary responsibility. And no easy task.

Raw ability guarantees nothing. Good ideas are abundant. Positive intention is not enough. Our potentialities need to be understood, developed and applied through focusing, organising, motivating, managing, continuously improving, and occasionally reinventing or transforming ourselves.

This is a skill in and of itself. A skill we're not born with, but one that must be learned if we are to find our own path, make the contribution and have the impact we want, and achieve happiness and success on our own terms.

How can 'Life Edge' help you?

'Life Edge' provides game-changing insights and a complete and coherent, field-proven, time-tested, practical and straightforward framework and approach that will enable you to take greater control. It will help you to:

- Develop a goal-setting system and use it to define your vision, values, and goals: aims that inspire you and keep you motivated

- Create a goal-achievement system that brings a consistent and disciplined focus on getting things done and on continually developing and improving across all aspects of life

- Develop a strong, positive mindset of proactivity, continuous improvement and resilience

Key principles

Self-management principles, tools and techniques help us to win the 'inner game'. This means mastering the ability to:

- Think clearly, positively and effectively so that we can choose our direction and priorities and use our time and energy wisely

- Manage our emotions (being aware of them and how they affect us, exercising self-control, and being positive, determined and resilient)

- Maintain a healthy and productive self-discipline

- Understand our strengths, develop them and put them to good use

Introduction

- Access flow – the state where we are simultaneously enjoying what we are doing and are highly productive, spontaneous and inspired

- Continually learn, adapt, evolve and grow emotionally, intellectually, behaviourally and spiritually (including mastering 'double loop learning' – getting better at getting better)

With practice and persistence, these principles will help you to spiral upwards towards increasingly greater capability, confidence, clarity of vision, and proactivity. Leveraging these significant, lasting and compounding benefits will give you a significant advantage at work and in wider life.

Mastering these meta-skills (skills that unlock other skills) provides a strong foundation for winning the 'outer game' – being able to excel in your chosen field and being able to collaborate with, and influence, others to achieve the results and the reputation you desire.

Figure 1 Winning the Inner Game

Getting started and keeping going

Being able to lead, manage and develop ourselves effectively is the secret of success in any domain. It's what separates the doers from the talkers and dreamers. But despite a long history of highly successful, ardent devotees and proven benefits, it's a still a minority pastime. Only about 4% of people (those who are committed to their personal growth, improvement and getting the best from themselves) do it to any serious degree. Why so?

People will struggle if they:

- Don't have a goal-setting process, and as a result, have not defined a compelling purpose, values and goals to give themselves a clear and motivating direction

- Don't have a goal-achievement process, a way to review progress, stay on track and learn from successes and setbacks. As a result, their efforts are haphazard, inconsistent and unsustained, so that the work they put in doesn't consistently translate into forward motion

- Have a passive or negative mindset, believing that they don't have the time to manage and develop themselves. That it's too hard, a waste of time, or won't work

The biggest barrier is that most people don't know how to go about building the goal-setting and goal-achievement systems and developing a strong, positive mindset. They don't have the tools, techniques, guidance or support to get started and to evolve it into a habit that brings lifelong benefits. It's not generally taught in schools, colleges, universities or workplaces, and most of the self-help books communicate the broad principles but offer neither the practical tools nor ongoing support to establish, embed or maintain the practice.

Introduction

People need a well-designed programme built on established wisdom and time-tested tools and techniques (rather than gimmicks or fads) to solve these problems and save them years of false starts and trial-and-error learning. That's what this book sets out.

Why it matters

> *"Inside every old person there is a young person wondering what the hell happened."* **(Terry Pratchett)**

Time is short. And it flies by. As Bodil Jönsson pointed out, if we live to the current average life expectancy of 81.5 years, we have "30,000 days and nights. That is our capital". Our energy is also limited. There are many routine demands on us, and also many other exciting possibilities. It's too easy for life to run away with us and for us to end up not enjoying the journey as much as we might, and not reaching as good a destination as we could.

Developing the capability to lead, manage and develop yourself is the path to personal and professional excellence. It gives you a positive and productive means of travelling and takes you to a better destination, and it helps you to make the most of your time and talents, maintain a balanced life, enjoy good physical and mental health, and achieve what you want at work and in your wider life. It confers advantages that grow cumulatively over a lifetime.

These skills are also the basis for leadership effectiveness. If you aspire to lead others, and help them to focus, organise, motivate, manage and continuously improve, you'll first need to master these skills yourself.

Life Edge

This book outlines a set of principles, tools and techniques for helping you lead, manage and develop yourself. It comprises three parts:

- Part one looks at the key concepts you need to know before taking practical action so that you can get the best from it
- Part two introduces the tools and some exercises to help you start using them
- Part three looks at how to establish the disciplines and embed these as a habit that delivers lifelong benefits

Overview

As with every form of excellence, personal or business, there is a process at the heart of leading, managing and developing yourself, underpinned by simple habits and routines. This process is outlined below.

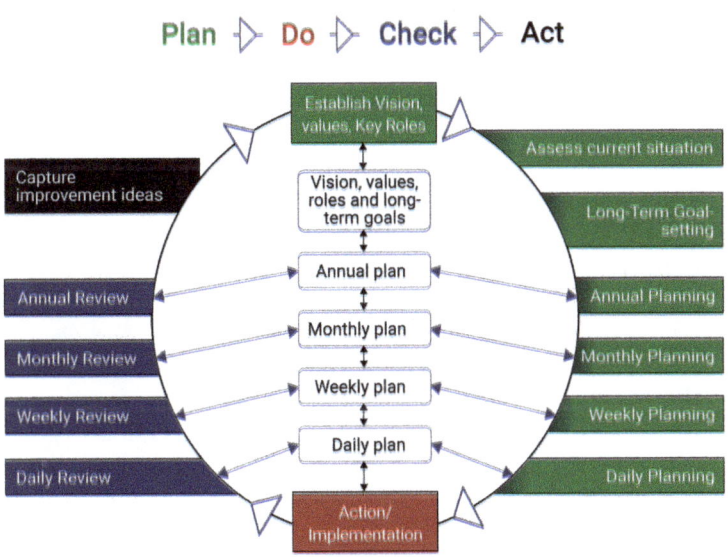

Figure 2 Personal Strategy Process Overview

Establish your mission, vision, etc

The first step is to identify your overall vision, purpose, values and key life roles, to create a sense of the big picture, the overall balance and the criteria against which you will measure life success.

Assess the current situation

The next step is to take stock and ascertain what is currently going well and where possibilities and opportunities for improvement lie.

Develop the long-term goals

In this step, the broad long-term goals for each key life-role are set.

Develop the cascade from the annual plan to monthly, weekly and daily objectives.

Next, the objectives for the coming year are developed and progressively cascaded into shorter-timescale plans and more concrete actions, from annual action plans to monthly, weekly and finally daily ones.

Implementation

The plans are actioned.

Review cascade from daily, through weekly and monthly to annual

Action and progress against the daily goals are reviewed, reflected upon and learned from, and at the same time, the next day's goals are set. At the end of the week a similar process is followed to review weekly goals and look ahead, then the same for each month, and then for the year as a whole. These progressively broader reviews maintain focus on the big picture, linking short-term actions, long-term goals and overall mission/purpose and values. Broader themes and trends in attitude, behaviour and performance can be identified and addressed.

The annual review looks at action, progress, results and the current position. It recognises and celebrates success to build confidence and identify the winning strategies that you want to continue, and to build on. It also generates learning points that can be taken forward into the following year's planning, on the:

- Content of the plan
- Execution of the plan
- Planning and implementation process

Improvement ideas captured

The lessons learned, on content, planning and the implementation process, are applied: adjustments are made prior to the start of the next cycle to ensure that the process continually improves and evolves.

Then the process repeats...

Part One

Leading, Managing And Developing Yourself – Key Concepts

Key concepts

PDCA (Plan-Do-Check-Act) thinking

"Our goals can only be reached through a vehicle of a plan, in which we must fervently believe, and upon which we must vigorously act. There is no other route to success." **(Pablo Picasso)**

Leading, managing and developing yourself is a goal-setting and goal-achievement process based on the PDCA cycle:

- **Plan:** Set out what success looks like for you, and your strategy for achieving it
- **Do:** Take action. Follow the plan

- **Check:** Review. Reflect on the reasons for any variance from the plan. Set out next actions. Draw encouragement from what went well. Learn from what did not

- **Act:** Act on lessons learned, make adjustments to the plan (the goals, the method or the success measures)

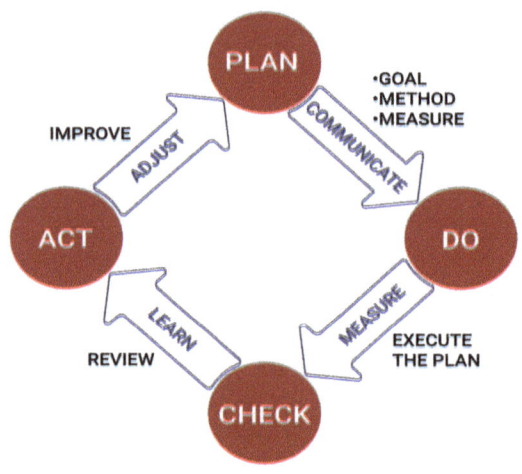

Figure 3 Plan-Do-Check-Act

This creates an upward spiral of consistent achievement and improvement, building powerful momentum as we cycle through these steps again and again. It is simple and universal. It is the same process that an Olympic athlete, or anyone serious about achieving their potential, will use. Only the content and depth of the goals and the intensity of the practice will vary.

Work smart: focus on effectiveness, not effort

> *"Doing more things faster is no substitute for doing the right things."* **(Stephen Covey)**

Part One

Effectiveness, achieving one's aims, inevitably requires effort and for that effort to be efficiently and skilfully executed. But time and effort, no matter how efficiently applied, count for little if spent on the wrong things.

The key is getting the balance right between:

- **Value-adding time:** Activities that directly contribute to the outcomes we want

- **Value-enabling time:** The planning, organising, reflecting, resting, relaxing, recharging and renewing required to optimise the impact of the value-adding time

- **Wasted time:** This includes time spent solving problems that could have been prevented; time frittered away on pointless distraction, procrastination or perfectionism; or time spent in ways that set you back – for example, doing poor-quality work that fails to have the intended impact or that needs redoing

Value-Adding
Design, build, assemble, pick, deliver
Value-Enabling
Planning, communicating, managing and developing people, process-improvement
Waste
Avoidable errors, working on the wrong priorities. Working inefficiently

Figure 4 Three ways of spending time

Value-enabling activities have the highest leverage, giving us the best ratio of time invested to results achieved. They narrow down what we need to do to an achievable amount of the most important things, and help us plan and prepare to do them well.

There is an interactive relationship between the three. Enough value-enabling time needs to be regularly invested, and spent wisely and efficiently. This can create an upward spiral of improving performance and capability. But with insufficient or poorly executed value-enabling time, waste increases and the amount and quality of value-adding time suffers, leading to getting stuck or entering a downward spiral.

The biggest challenge is to resist the emotional pull of the immediate and urgent and to invest enough quality time on the vitally important, but never urgent, value-enabling time. Which requires…

Self-discipline

> *"Success requires the continuous application of intelligent and directed effort."* **(Guy Browning)**

Self-discipline is the ability to maintain good habits and practices and deliver on the promises that we have made to ourselves and others.

Self-discipline is vital, since substantive achievements and consistently high-level performance tend not to come through having a sudden notion and making one big push. They come from an ongoing process of consolidating and building on many marginal improvements over a period of time. Like marathon running, what determines success is the steady discipline that goes into the build-up, not just one morning's heroic efforts.

Self-discipline is a high-level skill that can be learned, developed and improved, allowing us to continually enhance our ability to make bigger breakthroughs faster, and to sustain high-level performance. It thus confers a lifelong advantage.

Keep score

> *"First we need to figure out what winning looks like."* **(Bill Clinton)**

To successfully manage ourselves, we need to decide what winning looks like. Having something meaningful to aim for motivates and helps us persist through moments of difficulty and doubt. We also need a way to measure our progress, gauge the distance between us and our destination and figure out our next steps.

Given that it is our life and career, we are of course responsible for deciding what success looks like: what matters most to us, what the dimensions of success are and what level of achievement we are aiming for.

Take control

> *"You must not, ever, give anyone else the responsibility for your life."* **(Mary Oliver)**

Where we believe control of our life resides is something that profoundly influences our thinking, behaviour and results. An internal locus of control means operating in what Covey called our 'Circle of Influence'. It means taking responsibility, looking for what we can control and influence. Starting from where we are, doing what we can with what we've got. Thinking, deciding and acting for ourselves, and meeting life, as far as possible, on our terms. In this space we become more confident and ambitious, and we are also more likely to attract goodwill and support from others; "God loves a trier," as they say.

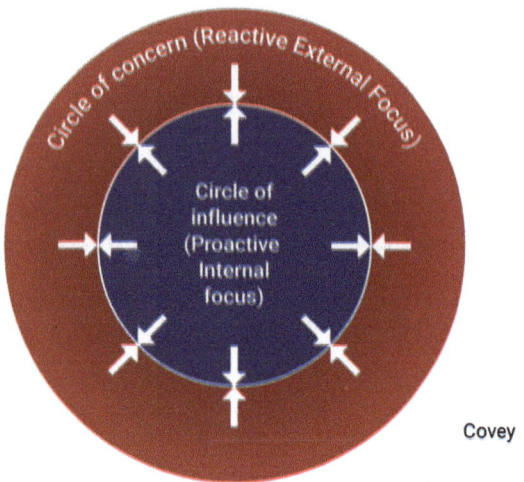

Figure 5 Locus of Control

With an external locus of control – what Covey called the 'Circle of Concern' – our minds gravitate towards things we can't directly control: problems, limitations, frustrations and barriers. This leads us towards negative thinking; worrying, criticising, complaining, blaming circumstances and other people for our situation (including our failure to act), and looking to others (usually the people we are blaming) to alleviate our problems. We focus more on coming up with excuses for failure and inaction than we do on finding possible solutions.

This can be psychologically appealing because it offers a way to evade responsibility, requires little effort or risk and avoids the difficulty of having to face anything, admit anything or change anything. But pinning our hopes on somebody else turning up to listen to our complaints, take responsibility and alleviate our problems is to look for an unlikely miracle.

It also weakens us, sapping our constructive energies and sense of agency, making us feel more helpless and despairing. And it invariably becomes a self-fulfilling prophecy and a trap that gets harder to escape. Furthermore, since it usually tells people more about the state of our mind than the state of reality, we can lose credibility. Nobody goes out their way to help someone who habitually moans and complains.

In short, living in the Circle of Influence expands our influence as our confidence, credibility, capability and results improve. Living in the Circle of Concern shrinks our influence as these things diminish.

Take control of your destiny or someone, or something, else will.

Be positive and proactive

> *"What most characterises immature people is that they sit around complaining that life doesn't meet their demands. What characterises the relatively few who are mature is that they regard it as their responsibility – even an opportunity – to meet life's demands."* **(M. Scott Peck)**

Taking control requires positivity and proactivity. Positivity is the ability to see what is there, what can be done, and to find a way forward – regardless of how challenging the situation is. Proactivity is making things happen, taking responsibility, taking action, influencing events.

Positivity – being optimistic and hopeful, talking a good game and constantly acquiring new insights and tools – is a good start, but without proactivity, nothing happens. Proactivity makes success more likely – to the degree that our efforts are skilfully planned and executed. Over time, the successes that come from being positive and proactive build confidence and ambition and create an upward spiral of greater achievement and action-orientation.

Mindfulness

> *"I am able to control only that which I am aware of. That which I am unaware of controls me. Awareness empowers me."* **(Sir John Whitmore)**

Attention is a powerful resource. Actions tend to follow where our attention goes. Also, if we focus on something consistently, we get more drawn into it, ramping up the intensity of that focus (for better or for worse).

It is of course too easy to get distracted, for our attention to be taken by something rather than given to it, so maintaining mindful awareness and directing and sustaining our attention on the right things is a skill worth developing. It has a significant impact on what we do and the results we get. Managing attention well is the skill that keeps our mind firmly in the Circle of Influence.

There are three different timescales across which we should be mindful of our focus and actions:

- Keeping our long-term values, purpose and goals front and centre
- Concentrating, and achieving flow, when a high level of task performance is required
- Being aware of our thoughts and emotions moment to moment. Noticing when our focus slips, distraction or head-trash (random thoughts, worries about half-finished jobs, etc) creeps in, and quickly refocusing ourselves on doing excellent work

Mindfulness is becoming an increasingly important skill as modern life brings new challenges. The sheer speed and amount of information that comes at us and the constant stimulation may detrimentally affect our ability to maintain concentration. The ready availability of information may blind us to the importance of developing mastery – building deep knowledge, insight and wisdom, problem-solving skills and systems thinking. All of these are high-leverage skills that require patience, reflection and original thinking. Life purpose, meaning and goals can only be derived through a mindful process. And without goals to orient us and define what success means to us, no amount of information will help us make substantive progress.

Review and reflect

Reviewing and reflecting on performance is invaluable for time management, maintaining work-life balance, managing stress and fostering personal growth. It helps you to:

- Recognise your strengths and take confidence and encouragement from them
- Recognise your mistakes, failures, limitations and weaknesses, keep them in proportion, learn from them and figure out how to develop beyond them or find other ways to compensate

- Translate what you have learned into appropriate positive action
- De-stress to get perspective on the troubles of the day, create a plan and not be kept awake dwelling on problems
- Enhance your emotional intelligence. Reflection is central to developing greater self-awareness and control over your attitude, behaviour and state of mind

Reflection is the mental and spiritual equivalent of turning on the windscreen wipers or cleaning your glasses. It brings clarity to how you see things and facilitates more insightful analysis, problem-solving and goal-setting.

Reflection does not mean sitting in the dark waiting for divine inspiration, it's about asking yourself a set of intelligent questions, connecting with that "still small voice" of inner wisdom. It brings you insights you would not otherwise have acquired and allows you to make better decisions. All of which will save you hours of wasted time and effort and take you to places you would not otherwise reach.

Ongoing personal development

"The only real security that one can have in this world is a reserve of knowledge, experience and ability." **(Henry Ford)**

The scope of our developmental aims should encompass all lines and all levels.

Lines of development are the different domains that, together, constitute a full and balanced life:

- Physical health and wellbeing
- Intellectual

- Emotional
- Spiritual
- Moral
- Behavioural
- Relational/social
- Real-world impact

Levels represent the degree of capability maturity, or 'vertical' development, for each line. There are various vertical development models, but they all follow three broad stages:

- Pre-conventional: Having no intrinsic interest in developing in that domain. Wanting to do as little as possible and only improving if compelled to, reluctantly and to the minimal degree
- Conventional: Will develop in ways that conform to, and reach the level of, social norms. For example, may study to gain a qualification but not maintain an interest in further development beyond that
- Post-conventional: Being intrinsically motivated to learn and improve, to learn in one's own way, bringing original thinking to the interpretation and application of what was learned and aspiring to self-determined high standards of excellence in knowledge, understanding and performance

In choosing what to prioritise for development, the first thing to do is ensure that we are not 'holed below the waterline' in any domain, i.e. in possession of a weakness so severe that it might sink the whole enterprise. (A weakness is where we have a limitation in an area we are required to perform well in. For example, not being able to sing might be a limitation, but it's not a weakness until we decide we want to be a vocal performer.) In the unlikely event that we do have a waterline issue, addressing this would be a priority. Beyond that, spending time working on our limitations will have little impact on our results and so might not represent the best use of our short and precious development time and resources.

Our biggest opportunity to excel is to focus on our strengths. First, identify your existing strengths and play to them, including any hitherto unrecognised, unused or underemployed strengths. Bring more of them into play. Then identify an area of strength that, if further developed, would make you especially valuable at work or bring particular benefits or satisfaction in your wider life. Work on that to elevate it to a high-level ability, a 'superpower' that makes a differential impact in areas of performance that directly relate to your key roles and goals.

Rest and renew

> *"Nobody on his deathbed ever said 'I wish I had spent more time on my business'."* **(Rabbi Harold Kushner)**

When we're working hard and there are many competing demands on our time, it's too easy to slip into the habit of grinding away endlessly and not getting the right amount or quality of rest. Rest is a crucial part of the performance equation. If you're stressed out and tired, it's hard to either perform well, enjoy what you're doing or improve. One argument is that episodes of peak performance will only be as high as the preceding valley of rest, recovery and preparation is deep. Or, as the old saying goes, "All work and no play makes Jack a dull boy".

So, first, it is important to schedule sufficient time to reflect, relax and recharge and trigger the parasympathetic nervous system, the body's 'rest and digest' response that facilitates deep recovery and renewal. One insidious effect of physical and psychological exhaustion is that it can overtake you and make you feel too tired for exercise, social interaction or hobbies. But these are all essential for staying in peak physical and mental shape. Making the decision that you will commit to them when your mind is clear and sharp, and scheduling them in advance, makes it more likely that you'll do them.

Second, give thought to the quality and balance of that time. It should encompass a range of activities that collectively refresh and renew. There may be a time and place for 'vegging out', but it is better to favour active rather than passive leisure. Passive leisure tends not to renew you but instead leads to 'psychic entropy', feeling listless and tired. More active leisure pursuits promote psychological detachment from work, create energy and enhance concentration, engagement and motivation, a sense of enjoyment and achievement, and feelings of control and mastery.

Self-management: why bother?

> *"The difference between great people and everyone else is that great people create their lives actively, while everyone else is created by their lives."* **(Michael Gerber)**

Avoid the pitfalls of not taking a structured approach

Not taking a systematic and structured approach to managing our work and wider life priorities runs the risk of making the journey harder, less enjoyable and less productive than it could have been, and not getting as far as our potential could have taken us.

The biggest danger is that, without defining our own success criteria and creating a plan and a process for executing it, we relinquish control of our time, direction and destiny. We open ourselves up to spending our time and energy working on someone else's dream, being drawn into dealing with other people's problems and dramas, working to someone else's idea of what we should do with our life and generally being at the mercy of events, carried where the currents take us.

We may also potentially:

- Lack focus, drive and motivation

- Become a 'busy fool': disorganised and inefficient, creating avoidable problems for ourselves and ending up putting in more time and effort than necessary while having less impact than desired

- Lack tenacity and persistence in pursuing goals, be easily knocked off track and unable to get any real momentum behind our improvement efforts

- Lose credibility with others at work and beyond. People (including ourselves) don't see us as capable of mustering the focus, organisation and discipline to achieve bigger and better things

- Experience poor job (and life) satisfaction, self-doubt, and demoralisation and frustration, feeling that we never get enough time to do everything we want, or to do anything as well as we would like

- Miss important opportunities. Many things will not be envisioned, far less achieved without forward thinking and planning

- Plateau: get to a certain level and no further, despite putting in a lot of work and effort
- Not achieve our full potential or get the rewards and satisfaction our time, effort and talent warrant

Reap the benefits of getting it right

With a structured approach to leading, managing and developing ourselves, we are more likely to:

- Be more focused and in control
- Do what we say we will do and deliver on the promises we make to ourselves and others
- Experience less stress and frustration
- Use time effectively
- Achieve more
- Enjoy a greater sense of accomplishment, satisfaction and peace of mind
- Have greater credibility at work and beyond
- Have more time for family, friends and relaxation
- Be generally more happy and productive
- Be ready when opportunity comes. As Roy Chapin says, "Luck is the time when preparation and opportunity meet"
- Gain a competitive edge: at the top of every field, things are decided by fine margins. John Hess said: "A race horse that can run a mile a few seconds faster is worth twice as much. That little extra proves to be the greatest value." So it is with people in competitive environments.

And there's no neutral zone, no place where doing nothing means that we keep what we've got. We're either getting it right, and in a virtuous circle making headway, or in a stuck loop experiencing self-reinforcing problems. Fixity is destiny. So if the latter is the direction we're heading and we don't take steps to change, the future is likely to be more of the same.

Finally, if we are a leader (or aspire to lead), we need to help other people set goals and deliver on what they commit to, respond appropriately to mistakes and continually develop. And unless we are managing our performance and development and dealing with these things in and for ourselves, we are unlikely to acquire the skills, sensibilities, insights, experience and credibility to lead others in any authentic, meaningful sense.

Achieving success begins with mindfulness, self-discipline, and recognising the importance of rest and balance in your life. It's time to focus on what matters most and lead your life with positivity and purpose. Now let's dive into the "How to" part.

Part Two

How To

Introduction: Practical steps to personal flourishing

'Life Edge' is of course an invitation to personal flourishing: to focus your life on your highest aspirations and possibilities. So the first step is for you to define what success looks like: to set out the future you want for you and your family.

The future that you will, sooner or later, live in is currently being shaped. But are you shaping it intentionally and purposefully, and if not, who or what is shaping it?

If you've read this far, you probably want your life to matter. You want to spend your time and energy well and for it to mean something to you, your family and others that your life touches now, in the future, and after you're gone.

When you actively envision this and plan the direction you choose to go, you'll set in motion a dynamic, lifelong process of positively engaging with life. The sense of possibility will excite and empower you, and sensitise you to emerging opportunities for action, development, improvement and progress. The action you take will bring learning, growth and achievement. This in turn builds your confidence and will whet your appetite to open up and explore future possibilities. Every turn of this spiral creates further reciprocal openings.

In short, your future, on your terms, is what you are investing in here.

Putting this into practice

To develop the techniques and tools to achieve your goals, you need to follow a two-step process:

- **Step one:** Creating a set of balanced life and work goals and your vision and values
- **Step two:** Establishing a routine for regular review and reflection

There is also the psychological aspect of establishing a positive and disciplined mindset that underpins the implementation of those goals.

Let's look at these in turn.

Step one: Top-level goal-setting

> *"Each one of us has to start out developing his or her own definition of success. And when we have these specific expectations of ourselves, we're more likely to line up to them. Ultimately, it's not what you get or even what you give, it's what you become."* **(Mary Gates)**

Because one can never build a life greater than its most noble purpose, it is important to start by setting out your highest and best aspirations. That is:

- Where you want to get to, and how you will bring the best of yourself to it

- Your personal vision of what you feel would add up to a life well lived, and what values and principles would guide your pursuit of this

- The outcomes you want, and who you are being while you are going about achieving them

Don't get sucked into aiming for something grandiose, abstract, overly heroic or couched in anyone else's terms. Aim for something that feels right for you. And bear in mind that what you write is not a lifelong commitment; it will evolve as you take action, learn and grow.

Defining your key life roles

The process begins by addressing the most important question: what does a successful life look like to you? The first step is to create a dashboard capturing the roles in your life that, together, create a complete and balanced picture of the future you want. (We're using the term 'roles' broadly to include all formal and informal roles and other key activities and responsibilities that matter to you and in which you wish to invest your time and energy.) Activities that you find meaningful, enjoyable and intrinsically motivating, that together create the recipe for a fulfilling and satisfying life, meeting your various health, social, emotional, intellectual, material and spiritual needs.

These roles would typically include:

- Work

- Family

- Friends/social life
- Fitness/health/sport
- Creative activities/hobbies/pastimes/recreation

See Action 1 in the accompanying Workbook Action Pack. If you don't have a print copy, download it here (www.futurepositiveconsulting.com/Life-Edge).

You can sub-divide these as appropriate. For example, 'Work' could include your roles as a manager, a technical specialist and a colleague. 'Family' could include your roles as a brother/sister, daughter/son, mother/father, etc.

Once you have the main headings, for each role, capture the broad detail and the emotional flavour of what success in that role looks and feels like to you.

Look ahead as far as you reasonably can: perhaps imagine that you've retired and someone asks you, "What were you most proud to have achieved?" Capture your thoughts on that. Usually, your first thoughts are the best. Sometimes, answers drop right into place. Most often it's an iterative process of getting each part right and then assessing how they all fit together to create a balanced and appealing whole. Perfection in this is neither possible nor necessary. Just get to a good place to start and the review system (described overleaf) will evolve and hone it as things unfold.

Having set the long-term goal in each area, capture what you aim to do this year. Make it a decent stretch but don't over-reach. You'll just set yourself up for frustration and disappointment if you do.

Once you have all the goals written down, you can check that the balance looks right across them all. Make sure that:

- All the right things are included

- There is not too much in there and everything can be given enough time and attention to allow it to be done enjoyably and successfully

- It adds up to satisfaction and doesn't just set you up for racking up accomplishments that won't necessarily lead to fulfilment. (Sometimes, high achievers don't use their prodigious drive wisely; this can lead to exhaustion and a sense of never being satisfied, and have negative consequences for other aspects of life such as health and relationships)

- Rest, recovery and relaxation are plumbed in. Explicitly. One insidious effect of exhaustion is that it can overtake you, making you feel too tired to muster the energy needed for exercise, social interaction or hobbies. But these are crucial to renewal and balance so should be prioritised, planned, committed to in advance and stuck to

It should feel like you're set up for a positive and exciting adventure. If not, go back and adjust your dashboard until it does.

Vision and values

Next, give some thought to what unites and coheres all of this.

> *"More than any other factor, vision affects the choices we make and the way we spend our time."* **(Stephen Covey)**

Using Action 2 on Vision and Values in the Action Pack, first set out your vision. This is literally what you set your sights on achieving in life. What you aspire to, the destination that you are trying to reach, your "Definite Major Purpose", as Napoleon Hill calls it. The 'ends'.

Then capture your values. These are, literally, what you value. What you stand for. What is important to you in your attitudes and behaviour. What you think will get you to where you want to go, while being the person you want to be: the 'means'. They define your method of travelling and provide personal standards that you can gauge yourself against.

Don't fall into the trap, with either of these, of thinking you have to write something dramatic. Just capture what is meaningful for you. Ideally, it should be simple, practical, meaningful, actionable, real and powerful. Make sure that your vision and values are ambitious enough (don't undersell yourself) and that they capture what is unique, special and meaningful for you. There are some examples overleaf.

Part Two

Example one:	Example two:	Example three:
Vision: To create a consistently successful team that serves clients and provides jobs worth having, while living a balanced life, succeeding as a father, partner, runner, friend and family member. To leave everyone and everything better than I found it. Values: • Be my own person • Take the initiative • Make time for the important things • Do good work with good people • Stay fit and healthy • Look for the positives in people and situations • Be home in time for weekends and birthdays	Vision: I'll leave every situation better than I found it. Values: • Treat everyone with dignity and respect • See everyone's possibilities and use their talents for everyone's benefit • Help others win • Develop people to be better than me • Work smart: do less and less to achieve • Value my time and energy and invest it wisely • Act with integrity • Be positive: always look for what can be done • Listen to others, create relationships • Learn, develop	Vision: To be the best I can be and help others be the best they can be. Values. • Think for myself • I will live my life fully, without preventing anyone from living their life fully • Take personal responsibility for my attitude and behaviour • Stay balanced and enjoy a full life • Be open to learning • Be positive • Continuously learn and improve • Look for, create and act on opportunities • Make a meaningful professional contribution • Be trusted

As with the roles exercise, just record your current thoughts. There are no right or wrong answers and this is something you can evolve gradually as life unfolds and you learn more, change, feel differently about things and, occasionally, reinvent when new opportunities and challenges appear.

Identify your breakthrough goal (optional)

With this all in place, you might choose, for the year ahead, to pick out the one goal that will make the biggest contribution to your overall long-term progress and set you up well for further advances. It should literally be a breakthrough, something that pushes you to a new level of skill, performance, confidence, achievement and satisfaction, either by going further in an existing direction or broadening out into new areas. It could be:

- A new, or much-postponed, positive life ambition
- A change that the time has come to make
- A work-related goal you need to achieve before time slips by or someone else claims the opportunity
- A stretch goal, building on your successes, confidence and reputation
- Overcoming some self-limiting thoughts, feelings (such as anxieties, fears or insecurities) or behaviours that are holding you back.

Quick summary of Step one

Together, your vision, values and goals should capture your broad aspirations, specific measures of success, and a sense of how you will get there. The end result should be something actionable against which you can measure progress and keep yourself on track.

This might be the most important piece of paper in your life – the blueprint of the future you want, with all the important ideas in one place.

Step two: Goal-achievement: regular planning, taking action, reviewing, reflecting and adjusting

Goal-achievement follows the PDCA (Plan-Do-Check-Act) cycle. It works best when we:

- Break down the broad aims into goals for progressively shorter time periods (month, week, day) to get to concrete action points
- Take the action that we committed to
- Review, learn, adjust and make course-corrections regularly, in a disciplined way

Let's look at the steps in the goal-achievement cycle and the tools that support and power it.

Plan

> *"Every minute you spend in planning saves as many as ten minutes of execution. It takes only around ten minutes to plan your whole day and you can save about two hours per day in execution, and be working on higher-leverage activities."* **(Brian Tracy)**

Planning is central to performance. Recall the old adage of the six Ps: Proper prior planning prevents poor performance!

Getting started

Begin by taking the goals you have set for each life role and map out the main milestones on the Annual Scorecard. (Action 3 in the Action Pack.) This should take about 15 minutes.

Now distil out from this your goals for the coming month in the Monthly Scorecard. (Action 4 in the Action Pack.) This should also take around 15 minutes.

There is of course a limit to how far it is possible to plan ahead with any degree of certainty, especially if we are doing something new or are in uncertain territory, so this month-by-month approach (which is contextualised within a yearly plan, which is in turn contextualised within our life goals) helps us go to the end of the torch beam – from where we can see further!

Ongoing planning process

At the start of each month, repeat this process of setting out your monthly goals. The same goes for each week. (See Action 5 in the Action Pack.) Planning a month or a week in broad detail takes about 10 to 15 minutes. Setting goals each day typically takes less than 10.

Once you have structured your goals and distilled them into weekly chunks, take the final step of picking out the key goals for the coming day. (Action 6 in the Action Pack.)

Develop the habit and discipline of starting every day by 'holding a meeting with yourself' to create or go over the plan.

When you do this, do it in a way that sets you up for success. Define the point that, if you reach it for any given day, week, etc, you'll be happy. Without defining a point at which you would be satisfied, you may never feel like you accomplish anything.

If this feels excessive, just ask yourself: how many days don't matter? For how many days a week is it okay to run the risk of not bringing the best of yourself to work and home situations? This daily routine is where the rubber hits the road. It keeps us focused on the succession of small steps that build the bigger, longer-term success, and ultimately shape our life and define our character.

It reminds us that we have 365 once-in-a-lifetime opportunities every year to act mindfully and rack up small but meaningful chunks of progress, and to incrementally and inexorably ratchet up our learning and capability. This builds into weeks, months and years where we register increasingly significant breakthroughs with increasing momentum as we move forwards through various challenges and difficulties to achieve our ambitions.

This daily planning and execution is the groundwork we do to be prepared when Lady Luck turns up and opportunities present themselves.

Some people never miss an opportunity to miss an opportunity! Don't be in that camp.

This fine-grain focus also allows us to be confident that, each day, our goals and actions will make the best use of our time and move us towards our long-term goal.

> *"When I forget to remind myself of what's really important, I find that I can quickly lose sight of my priorities and, once again, get lost in my own busyness. I'll rush out the door, work late, lose my patience, skip my exercise and do other things that conflict with the goals of my life."* **(Richard Carlson)**

This should, over time, create a sense of being in control from knowing that anything important has been captured so that your subconscious doesn't have to chunter away, worrying that you've missed something vital. It also has the effect of intensifying your focus on your goals. No matter how well we know something, seeing it in writing and seeing it repeatedly reinforces its impact and increases the probability of it getting done.

The very act of thinking and planning also unlocks your mental powers, triggers your creativity, and increases your mental and physical energies.

> *"When you are inspired by some great purpose ...*
> *dormant forces, faculties and talents become alive,*
> *and you discover yourself to be a greater person by far*
> *than you ever dreamed yourself to be."* **(Patanjali)**

You'll get the time invested back many times over, simply by not having to fix problems you avoided because you foresaw them. Planning is, after all, just making mistakes on paper to avoid making them in reality! And through this process, you'll get the benefit of seeing opportunities for greater efficiency and higher achievement that you would not otherwise have spotted.

Do

> *"Fill the unforgiving minute with sixty seconds'*
> *worth of distance run."* **(Rudyard Kipling)**

If it's in the plan, do it. You wrote it. It makes sense. Dive in. Get it done. The right time for action is now.

Also, aim, as far as possible, to get in, and stay in, a state of flow. Being 'in the zone' is where we simultaneously enjoy what we are doing and are highly productive, creative and spontaneous.

Spending too long in the comfort zone feels dull and delivers mediocrity. Pushing too hard for too long into overburden becomes counterproductive and leads to burnout – a significant long-term loss of motivation and capability.

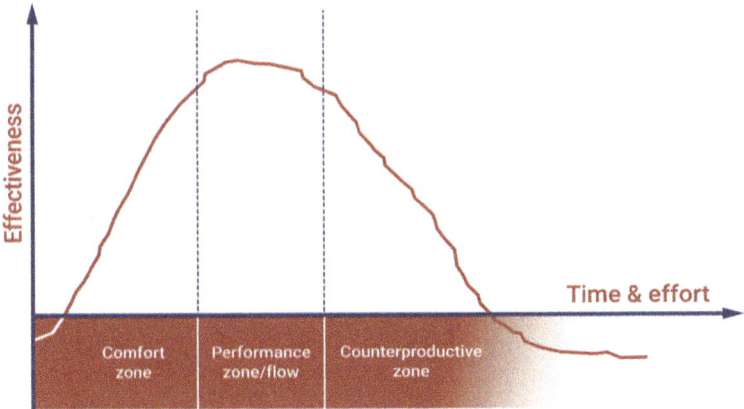

Figure 6 Effort vs Effectiveness

Within all of this, remember that sometimes, it is more about timing than time. It's *when* you perform, not just *how* you perform, so make sure, above all, that you show up in the moments of truth:

- Raise your game to win the big points and get things over the line in critical situations

- Maintain solid discipline and standards on uneventful days when it would be easy to become complacent and no one would notice if you let things slip

- Hang on in difficult moments when it would be easy to give up on your goal

Check

"If at first you don't succeed, find out why." **(Stephen Covey)**

Set up a routine for daily review, reflection, course-correction and adjustment (and for planning the next day). Do the same reviews at the end of each week and month. Schedule time to do this regularly rather than waiting for a setback to trigger reflection. As Richard Carlson says, "A low mood is not the time to analyse your life. To do so is emotional suicide."

The purpose of structured reflection is to review progress towards the goals you set and assess how well you are adhering to your personal values.

Daily review typically takes 10 minutes or less. Simply revisit your goals and ask yourself: what was *planned;* what was the *actual* outcome; what was the *variance;* what was the *reason* for the variance; what *action* is required to correct any immediate problem and improve the approach going forward. Action 6 in the Action Pack is also the tool for this.

Use the same approach for the weekly, monthly and yearly reviews. You can use Actions 7, 8 and 9 respectively in the Action Pack to focus these reviews and record the noteworthy points. Any significant improvement opportunities that you can't easily weave into your daily/weekly planning can be captured in Action 10, the Opportunities List. Ideas captured here can be built into the next monthly or annual plan at the appropriate point in the planning cycle.

Getting the right psychological approach to the review process is essential. Give yourself credit when you deserve it. Many people just skip to what didn't go right and miss this rare and invaluable opportunity to recognise positives, identify successful approaches and strategies, build authentic self-confidence and develop a sense of control.

And when things don't go right, don't beat yourself up. It's just counterproductive to waste your time and energy berating yourself for what's already done. Just be honest with yourself, note any shortfalls and try to identify the reasons for them. If, on occasion, you need to have an honest and constructive exploration of (say) a tendency to procrastinate, then do that to try and understand the reasons and identify action points, not to point up flaws and castigate and demoralise yourself.

Learn (or relearn!) what you can, and commit to any improvement action that might help you stay on the bike a bit longer before falling off the next time. Then come to terms with it and let it go. It's all about gradual, incremental progress. Perfection is neither possible nor necessary. Beating ourselves up and emerging with nothing other than a 'try harder' goal is usually neither productive nor especially developmental.

We are, of course, certain to make some mistakes over and over again. In some aspects of performance it is neither possible nor desirable to eradicate these because the issue is the 'shadow side' of a significant strength. For example, 'being too pedantic' may just be taking the strength of being good with detail slightly too far on particular occasions. Attempting to eliminate this would mean subduing that strength. In these instances, the check process acts in the immediate term as a 'rumble strip' to spot if things are going too far and make adjustments, and in the long term to help us learn to become more skilful at regulating these abilities.

"For years I have kept an engagement book showing all the appointments I had during the day. My family never made any plans for me on Saturday night, for the family knew that I devoted a part of each Saturday evening to the illuminating process of self-examination and review and appraisal. After dinner I went off by myself, opened my engagement book, and thought over all the interviews, discussions and meetings that had taken place during the week. I asked myself: What mistakes did I make that time? What did I do that was right – and in what way could I have improved my performance? What lessons can I learn from that experience?

I often found that this weekly review made me very unhappy. I was frequently astonished at my own blunders. Of course, as the years passed, these blunders became less frequent. Sometimes I was inclined to pat myself on the back a little after one of these sessions. This system of self-analysis, self-education, continued year after year, did more for me than any other one thing I have ever attempted. It helped me improve my ability to make decisions – and it aided me enormously in all my contacts with people. I cannot recommend it too highly." **(Andrew Carnegie)**

Meditation

Meditation is a way to powerfully augment 'check'. Meditation is the simple process of sitting comfortably and still and centring and focusing the mind. There are various approaches, including:

- Awareness of breathing: not trying to control the breath, just tuning in and relaxing into it

- Awareness of our thoughts: not hooking into them or reacting to them and being led down rabbit holes, just being aware of them and practising letting them rise and fall, come and go

- Focusing on a concept we aspire to develop more of – for example, patience or concentration

These approaches all help to reduce the 'head trash' and to relax and to gently calm the mind. Ten to 15 minutes is a good length of time to aim for to begin with.

This all helps deal with the stuff that usually wakes us up in the small hours, and helps us to get a more restful sleep and be more energised, focused and positive at the start of the following day.

Act

Follow through on any in-flight adjustments or longer-term changes you commit to. Build the bigger, more strategic changes into your plans. Action the smaller "kaizen" improvements immediately.

As John Harvey Jones observed, "Success is a series of corrected failures." That's why regularly cycling through these steps is invaluable. It allows you to take comfort and confidence from your progress, identify missteps and take timely action to get back on track. It helps, over time, to incrementally develop insight into, and gradually extinguish, tactical, emotional and behavioural approaches that don't work, and establish ones that work better. It also helps manage work-life balance and minimise stress, giving us a greater sense of control.

See Action 12 of the workbook for rating your Self-Management Competences.

Establishing and embedding this as a life habit

"The secret of your future is hidden in your daily routine."
(Mike Murdock)

The power of this process is in establishing and embedding it as a daily habit. The best way to do this is to create a simple timetable for reviewing and planning, and commit to it. A suggested timetable is given below and there is a blank template in Appendix 1 in the Action Pack for you to create your own.

Daily	Every day: review of day and planning for tomorrow. Scheduled for before evening wind-down activities. Augment by 15 minutes meditation before bedtime
Weekly	Sunday evening review: review of week and planning for the coming week. Scheduled for before evening wind-down activities. (Incorporates daily review)
Monthly	Last Sunday of month: review of month and planning for the coming month. Scheduled for before evening wind-down activities. (Incorporates weekly and daily review)
Mid-year	Last Sunday of June (or on return from annual holiday): review of first half of year and planning for the remainder. Schedule an hour or so where you can work uninterrupted
Annual	Last Sunday of year: review of the year and planning for the coming year. Schedule an hour or more where you can work uninterrupted

Part Two

Barriers

> *"Most of the good habits are common sense, but only one person in fifty is actually willing to do it."* **(Shia LaBeouf)**

There is nothing complex, strange or time-consuming about this process (indeed, you'll get your time back many times over). However, only around 2-4% of people have established it as a habit. The biggest barrier is that most people have not been taken through it.

Most of the barriers to following through are internal and psychological. Leading, managing and developing yourself involves four acts of courage that not everyone chooses to embrace: actively committing to our priorities; being accountable to ourselves; dealing with the insights that the review process reveals about our limitations and weaknesses; and letting go of old habits, scripts and attitudes that are comfortable and familiar, but limiting.

At the start, we may also have to deal with other people's attitudes. Sometimes, people around us feel threatened when we take control of our lives and offer discouragement, because if you succeed, they lose all their excuses for inaction. And trying to stop you is a lot easier than trying to develop themselves.

Where most people who fail, fail, however, is through simply not maintaining self-discipline around daily planning and review. Which is a shame, given the differential impact those 10 minutes per day have on what gets achieved in the other 1,430! It might seem like a trivial exercise, but like the coupling that links a locomotive to the train carriages, it is the small, apparently insignificant element that connects our ambitions to the engine that will turn them into reality: our organisational abilities, motivation, energy and creativity. The willingness to stick to this simple discipline is a strong indication of how serious we are about taking responsibility for our lives, and about developing and improving.

You may wish to pause here until you have completed the exercises in your workbook as it feeds into Part 3: Making it Work for You.

Part Three

Making It Work For You

So far, we've looked at the thinking behind how to successfully lead, manage and develop yourself and laid out some initial plans for what you want to do and how you'll go about it. It's now time to make the leap from thinking and planning to action.

To do this, you'll need two things: a good process and the right mindset.

Establish your process

Establishing a process for goal-setting and goal achievement is important. This process is the engine that makes it go. It shapes the goals and drives the implementation and continuous improvement. It is what we need to keep our vision, values and goals in view so that we stay focused, on track and moving forward. It also helps us to refine and refresh our aims regularly as circumstances change and we gain new insights and information.

Having such a process makes us smarter in three ways. It:

- Makes sure that we are working on the right priorities; the high-leverage activities that contribute meaningfully to our success

- Highlights when we're off track and what we need to do to fix it ('first loop learning')
- Helps us understand how we got off track and how we can avoid repeating the error ('second loop learning'). This also allows us to work with increasingly greater speed and precision

The quality of the process you develop and the discipline with which you follow it needs to be as important to you as your aims are.

Make sure that the timetable you set out earlier will generate the right intensity of focus and that you are emotionally committed to persevere with it until it starts working for you and becomes established as a habit.

Mindset

> *"Sooner or later, all motivation is self motivation."* **(Seth Godin)**

Your success in managing and developing yourself ultimately comes down to commitment and disciplined practice. This process needs to be as important to you as your hopes and dreams are. The right mindset is vital. This will include:

- Making the time. (Time won't be 'found')
- Quiet perseverance with the self-management process. Like a musician practising scales over and over, if you work conscientiously and mindfully, you will ratchet forward, incrementally building your skill and achieving a level of consistency. There will inevitably be times when your focus slips, but if you refocus and keep

going, those slips will become less frequent and less disruptive and you'll be rewarded with moments of breakthrough. Falling off the bike is inevitable; the trick is to learn how get back on faster and go further before falling off the next time, and to survive the whole journey through what Inger Mewburn called "the Valley of Shit", the period of struggle where we feel a loss of confidence and motivation before the breakthrough to success. Discipline is required at all times, especially in the early stages until it becomes a habit

- Dealing with issues that the process throws up. Some of these will require change at a fundamental level; for example, continually evolving your values, attitudes and behaviours. This can be hard. But meaningful growth and development is not possible without it. You will also inevitably have to work to overcome internal fears, self-doubts and insecurities as you push into unfamiliar and sometimes challenging territory. Personal change is more of a vision and courage thing, less of a time thing. It is small, courageous changes, such as sitting down with a difficult person, or confronting our own negative thinking or habits, that moves us forward, unlocks time and energy and builds the confidence to make further progress. As Hanley and Deville write, "Changes in behaviour do not come easily or quickly. In fact, change usually occurs in small doses, one step at a time"

- Remain positive and proactive. Keep setting and achieving stretch goals. This builds confidence and ambition and creates its own dynamic. Define yourself by your possibilities, not your fears or limitations

- Embrace life's inevitable challenges, setbacks and defeats. These are not defining moments in a negative sense (unless you let them be). What matters is what you do next. Facing and overcoming such difficulties is a necessary part of the process of developing insight, resilience and character. Indeed, it's probably the only way to develop insight, resilience and character. Make these positively defining moments. As Winston Churchill humorously observed, "Success is the ability to go from one failure to another with no loss of enthusiasm"

- Be committed but not attached: put in your best efforts, but don't be so attached to the result as to get deflated when things don't work out (which will be a fair bit of the time on the road to achieving high standards and ambitious goals)

- Play the long game. Success usually comes when opportunity meets preparation. Do the groundwork, and be alert to opportunities and take them when they arrive

Don't wait for the wake-up call

> *"Where the occasion and opportunity quietly offer, it is better than to wait for turbulent necessity."* **(Thomas Paine)**

Taking control, setting our own priorities, planning how to make the best use of our time and energy and grasping life's opportunities is something we can do any time. But too often, people are only spurred into it by a crisis or a setback that gives them a sharp wake-up call. And without this, many drift on and never confront their difficulties, take control and unlock their potential.

Acute short-term pain can be motivational, but dull ongoing dissatisfaction just corrodes belief and motivation. So don't wait for the wake-up call. It might not come, or it might come too late.

Grab hold of your life: don't just go through the motions, be working on a dream or vision that motivates and excites you.

Building and maturing our self-management capability

The process of managing and developing yourself can, at first, feel like an unnatural activity, then perhaps a bit of a chore. Then it becomes a conscious discipline, and finally a habit. As with all strategies for achieving excellence, the benefits really begin to accrue as our capability matures and we advance progressively through the different stages of the journey to established expertise and success:

- **Level 1 – Initial/ad-hoc:** Having no system and being reactive in our approach to managing our time and energy at work and in our wider life

- **Level 2 – Repeatable:** Having a basic approach that we apply only when we really need to

- **Level 3 – Defined:** Having a properly designed, complete and coherent system for managing our time and energy at work and in our wider life

- **Level 4 – Managed and focused:** Using the system with consistency and discipline

- **Level 5 – Optimised:** Fine-tuning the system and using it to help us identify, develop and realise the optimal life for us

Tip: Regularly checking in with Tool 12, Self-Management Competences is a useful way to gauge your progress.

Walk the path

"There's a difference between knowing the path and walking the path." **(Morpheus in The Matrix)**

There's nothing here that you couldn't do, nothing too complex, too hard or time-consuming. But it is a professional-level system, not a marketing gimmick promising instant success. As such, it will take at least a month to overcome inertia, settle into a pattern and begin to see some tangible results, and thereafter it requires ongoing discipline to maintain progress, to embed it as a habit and evolve it over time. There are no short cuts. But it works when you work.

Next Steps

"There is no silver bullet! However, there is an approach that is more powerful, more certain, and more reliable than any silver bullet. It's something that we all have the power to implement immediately and it almost always produces favourable results." **(Robert Middleton)**

Being able to lead, manage and develop yourself effectively is the secret of success in any domain. It might sound like common sense. But it's not common practice. Only 2-4% of people take a systematic and disciplined approach to it and consequently enjoy the consistent and sustained benefits that come from it.

This is because many people:

- Amid the noise and clutter of fads and trends develop, at best, a piecemeal and fragmented understanding of the area and can't find a place that they are confident enough in to stick with for any length of time

- Don't have a complete and coherent, field-proven, time-tested, practical and straightforward approach

- Will consequently struggle to develop the practices and form the habits that will enable them to get traction, and to maintain the focus, discipline and consistency required to translate their hopes and aspirations into meaningful and sustained progress

The good news is that we have tackled these issues so you don't have to.

'Life Edge' is the result of several decades of work during which we have done the research and built, field-tested and honed the framework, models, tools and techniques. This gives you, straight out of the box, a comprehensive, coherent, field-proven, time-tested strategy and approach – a huge advance on a loosely connected collection of tactics. It can save you years of false starts and frustrating trial-and-error learning.

It enables you to:

- Identify what success means to you: your vision, values, key life roles and goals

- Build a system for translating those aspirations into concrete action plans, then taking action, reflecting, learning and adjusting

- Develop the mindset to maintain discipline, overcome difficulties and continually develop. A mindset of ambition, willingness to take action, face and overcome difficulties and setbacks, building, over time, a robust winning mentality

When applied with discipline and consistency, this powerful, high-leverage approach brings significant, lasting and compounding lifelong benefits. There are, firstly, the significant cumulative advantages that accrue over a lifetime of using this approach, creating a significant gap between what you achieve with it and what would have happened without it.

Perhaps even more important is the benefit of having a robust means of navigating life's ever-changing landscape of opportunities and challenges. This increases your chances of living a balanced, successful and satisfying life, thriving in the good times and getting through the tough ones.

The approach outlined here is for you if you are serious about discovering and developing your best self and are prepared to take action. It will help you to find your direction and see what is possible and give you the confidence and practical strategies to take effective action, stay on track, and deal with setbacks, distraction, procrastination and other barriers to progress. It will help you to identify and unlock more of your potential and feel more focused and in control. It will get you closer to achieving the rewards that your time, talent and efforts deserve.

Are you up for it?

- Is there more you want than you are currently getting from life? Are there talents you want to unlock, challenges you want to take on, new capabilities you wish to develop, new heights you want to scale?

- Whose hands do you want your future to be in? Chance? Other peoples? Or your own?

- If you don't take control of your hopes, dreams, aspirations, time, decisions, actions and energy, but keep waiting for someone or something else to, what is likely to happen?

- If not this, what? If not now, when?

Time passes. If you are not happy with your situation or direction, it's time to draw a line. It's time to take control.

It's time

1. You are done with the frustrations and limitations of your existing approach
2. You have in your hands a coherent, field-proven, time-tested framework, system and approach that gives you a line of sight to real, sustained progress
3. You are ready to commit

Let's get to work.

Bonus Items

Bonus 1: If you haven't done so already, download your complimentary Action workbook.

Bonus 2: Download the Visual Data Companion to reinforce key learning points.

Bonus 3: Watch the bonus video with positive affirmations/quotes to keep you inspired and on track.

Just visit www.futurepositiveconsulting.com/life-edge

More From Life Edge

'Life Edge' – personal coaching

The 'Life Edge' personal coaching programme is designed to help you put these principles into practice and overcome barriers to progress. It can save you years of false starts and frustrating trial-and-error learning.

It is for people who are serious about discovering and developing their best self, and who are prepared to take action. It will help you to find your direction, and leave you with practical strategies tailored to you and the confidence you need to take that action, stay on track and deal with setbacks, distraction, procrastination and other progress blockers.

Up for it?

Ask yourself this:

- Is there more you want to get from life? Are there talents you want to unlock, challenges you want to take on, new heights you want to scale?

- Who do you want to control your future? Other people? Chance? Or you yourself?

- If you don't take control, what is likely to happen?

- If not this, what? If not now, when?

Time passes. If you are not happy with your situation or direction, then it's time to take responsibility for leading, managing and developing yourself and to take control of your future direction, success and happiness.

To learn more, get in touch via: https://futurepositiveconsulting.com/contact

About Future Positive Consulting

What we do

Founded in 1998, Future Positive consulting work in partnership with leaders who aspire to build organisations that are excellent places to work for, buy from, and invest in. Businesses which, through their products and practices add genuine and enduring value to customers, colleagues and the communities they work within.

How

Our 'Toward Excellence' toolkit provides a coherent and time-tested system for achieving business excellence; and has been built over three decades of research, practice, learning and refinement, working in partnership with clients on live challenges and opportunities. We use this and a combination of consulting, coaching, facilitation and training to help each business figure out their own approach to excellence and to implement, maintain and continuously improve it.

Our clients

The people we serve are serious about, and committed to, building a world class business. They are typically formative CEO's who are looking for a customised methodology, toolkit and specialist support to design and implement a bespoke approach to management that:

- Enhances long term business performance.
- Increases resilience, adaptive capacity and improvement capability.
- Fully utilises the knowledge, experience and capability of its people.

Our clients' companies vary in size from scale-ups defining culture and market position, to global organisations optimising cost and operational performance in fine-margin industrial environments.

The principles of business excellence are sector agnostic, this allows us to work with clients in a wide range of industries including tech, luxury goods, agriculture, financial services, pharmaceuticals, engineering and food retail distribution.

Discover more

Visit futurepositiveconsulting.com.

Bibliography

All are books unless otherwise noted.

- Shawn Achor: The Happiness Advantage
- James Allen: As a Man Thinketh
- Tom Butler-Bowden: 50 Success Classics
- Tom Butler-Bowden: 50 Psychology Classics
- Tom Butler-Bowden: 50 Self-Help Classics
- Richard Carlson: Don't Sweat the Small Stuff
- Clayton M. Christensen: How Will You Measure Your Life (Harvard Business Review paper)
- Stephen Covey: The 7 Habits of Highly Effective People
- Mihaly Csikszentmihalhi: Finding Flow: The Psychology of Engagement with Everyday Life
- Mihaly Csikszentmihalhi: The Evolving Self: A Psychology for the Third Millennium
- Anthony De Mello: Awareness
- Dr Wayne W. Dyer: You'll See It When You Believe It

Bibliography

- Tim Ferriss podcast: https://tim.blog/podcast/
- Viktor E. Frankl: Man's Search for Meaning
- Erich Fromm: To Have or To Be?
- W. Timothy Gallwey: The Inner Game of Tennis
- Shakti Gawain: Creative visualization
- Seth Godin blog: https://seths.blog/
- Daniel Goleman: Vital lies, simple truths
- Daniel Goleman: Emotional Intelligence
- Daniel Goleman: Working with Emotional Intelligence
- Charles Handy: The Empty Raincoat
- Dr Jesse Lynn Hanley and Nancy Deville: Tired of Being Tired
- Harald Harung: Improved Time Management through Human Development (Journal of Managerial Psychology)
- Harvard Business Review: https://hbr.org/
- Napoleon Hill: Think and Grow Rich
- Jon Kabat-Zinn: Mindfulness for Beginners
- Jon Kabat-Zinn: Wherever You Go, There You Are
- Robert Kegan: The Evolving Self
- Jiddu Krishnamurti: Think on These Things
- Alan Lakein: How to Get Control of Your Time and Your Life
- Jim Loehr, Tony Schwartz: The Making of a Corporate Athlete (Harvard Business Review paper)

- Abraham Maslow: The Farther Reaches of Human Nature
- Abraham Maslow: A Theory of Human Motivation
- Thomas Paine: Rights of Man
- Norman Vincent Peale: The Power of Positive Thinking
- M. Scott Peck: The Road Less Travelled
- Matthieu Ricard: Happiness: A Guide to Developing Life's Most Important Skill
- Matthieu Ricard: The Art of Meditation
- Carl Rogers: On Becoming a Person
- David Rooke and William R. Torbert: Seven transformations of leadership (Harvard Business Review paper)
- Brian Tracy: Change Your Thinking, Change Your Life
- Jonny Wilkinson: Tackling Life

www.ingramcontent.com/pod-product-compliance
Lightning Source LLC
Chambersburg PA
CBHW061234070526
44584CB00030B/4117